Clinton Scollard

Pictures in Song

Clinton Scollard

Pictures in Song

ISBN/EAN: 9783744769891

Printed in Europe, USA, Canada, Australia, Japan

Cover: Foto ©Thomas Meinert / pixelio.de

More available books at **www.hansebooks.com**

PICTURES IN SONG

BY

CLINTON SCOLLARD

———

NEW YORK & LONDON
G. P. PUTNAM'S SONS
The Knickerbocker Press
1884

TO

MY MOTHER.

These songs of mine like dews that gleam
Beneath the morning's crimson beam,
   May vanish, and be seen no more,
   But murmur round that unknown shore
Where those, the long forgotten, teem.

Yet list, I pray, and do not deem
That they are Fancy's idle theme,
   But pictures culled from Nature's store,
              These songs of mine.

For them no glory do I dream.
I only wish that they should seem
   Like little birds that softly pour
   Their low sweet notes out as they soar,
Or wandering rills from Tempe's stream,
              These songs of mine.

v

CONTENTS.

MADRIGALS.

	PAGE
By the Turret Stair	3
My Vis-à-Vis	5
Temptation	8
To a Chinese Idol	9
A Kerchief	11
Myrtis	12
Completion	14
Theft	16
Moorish Love Song	18
A Bit of Lace	19
"Mother Hubbard"	20
Teresa in the Garden	22

LYRICS AND LAYS.

Fort Marion	27
Hymn of the Pine	30
On a Bust of Antinous	32
To a Mocking Bird	35
Sappho	37
An Autumn Scene	39
Morning on the Mountains	40

CONTENTS.

A Fair Novice	42
Amid the Marshes	45
The Crocus	50
A Sprig of Heather	52
A Song for November	54
Reverie	58
Night on the Ochlawaha	60
Farewell and Hail	62
Retrospection	64
December	67
Theocritus	68
In the Mission Burial Ground	71
Herrick	72
An August Noon	74
A Lily of the Valley	77
The Sailing of the Sea Gull	80

BALLADES, ETC.

Ballade to Villon	91
Ballade of Dead Poets	93
Ballade for a Wedding	95
Ballade of the Bard	97
The Prayer of Dryope, (Rondeau Redoublé)	99
At Peep of Dawn, (Rondeau)	101
When Sirius Shines "	102
Vis Erotis "	103
"I Heard a Maid With Her Guitar," (Rondel)	104
" Upon the Stair I See My Lady Stand," (Rondel)	105
A Snowflake in May, (Triolet)	106

In the Sultan's Garden, (Pantoum)	107
Villanelle to Helen	110
Villanelle to the Daffodil	112
Cupid and the Shepherd, (Sestina) . . .	114
On Receiving a Plaque of Apple-Blossoms, (Huitain) .	117
On a Picture of Orpheus Playing before Pluto, (Dizain)	118
King Boreas, (Chant Royal)	119

SONNETS.

The Lute Player	125
Dawn	126
Twilight	127
Moonrise	128
Midnight	129
The Coming of the Goddess	130
A Vision of Pain	131
At Easter Vespers	132
Discovery	133
A Lock of Hair	134
"Le Roi est Mort; Vive le Roi." . . .	135
Priscilla	136
Aganippe	137

MADRIGALS.

I

BY THE TURRET STAIR.

(A. D. 1200.)

Run ! run ! little page, tell your lady fair
That her lover waits by the turret stair,
That the stars are out, and the night-wind blows
Up the garden path from the crimson rose—
>Run ! run ! little page.

Haste ! haste ! little page, ere the round moon's rim
Peeps over yon edge of the forest dim,
And the breeze has died which seems to bear
The scent of the rose from the trellis there—
>Haste ! haste ! little page.

Soft ! soft ! little page, lest her sire may guess,
By her look of fear and of fond distress,
That he hides in the night by the turret stair

Who would steal from his bower the flower so fair—
   Soft ! soft ! little page.

List ! list ! little page, to that faint footfall
Far away in the depths of the vaulted hall !
Is it echo alone, or a mournful moan
Borne out from those ghostly walls of stone ?
   List ! list ! little page.

See ! see ! little page, who stands in white
All clad in the pale and changing light !
Is 't an angel ? ay, 't is my lady fair,
And she hastes to her love down the turret stair—
   See ! see ! little page.

Farewell ! little page, for away, away,
Through the still black night to the dawn of day,
My lady so sweet and I must fare
Till we reach the foot of *my* turret stair—
   Farewell ! little page.

MY VIS-À-VIS.

From my airy casement high,
Far above the passers-by,
    I can see,
Just across the thoroughfare,
Such a charming debonair
    Vis-à-vis.

I know not the maiden's name,
Yet my lips will often frame
    Names as sweet
As the little mating birds
Nigh articulate in words,
    And repeat.

Is it Ethel? Is it Rose?
Is it Isabel?—who knows?
    Would I knew!

MY VIS-À-VIS.

Ah! she looks demure and wise
With her long-lashed, downcast eyes,
    They are blue!

But she pays not slightest heed
While I watch her sit and read
    By the hour;
Little dreams she that I'm near,
And still less that I dare peer
    In her bower.

Would I might contrive to look
Into that absorbing book,
    Pretty maid!
Is it Byron? Is it Scott?
Is it—but I know it's not—
    Witty Praed?

'T is a tale of love, perchance,
Or some thrilling old romance
    Of the days
When the gallant knight and lord

Won at joust, with lance and sword,
    Ladies' praise.

Had we lived in that far time,
When gay troubadours in rhyme
    Sang of love,
Then I might have been her knight,
And into the tourney-fight
    Worn her glove.

But to-day I only know
She is very fair, and so
    This be said—
Ever may good luck attend;
I will be her unknown friend—
    Till she's wed!

TEMPTATION.

'Mong rings, and other dainty things,
    Within a casket pink and pearly,
It lies beneath my longing eyes,
    This tempting treasure soft and curly.

And faint a mocking-bird makes plaint
    Beside the snowy-curtained casement,
While there, within a picture fair,
    A novice bows in meek abasement.

There's no one here to see, and so
    Why should I hesitate or falter?
I, too, would kneel and swear me true
    Were this bright ringlet on the altar!

But list!—a step—I must resist.
    The proverb says, (and all men know it,)
A thief will surely come to grief,
    And none abide a thievish poet!

TO A CHINESE IDOL.

Once you ruled, a god divine,
In a sacred shady shrine
Near a river dark as wine
    'Mid the trees,
And to you the mandarins,
With their smooth unshaven chins,
Prayed absolvence from their sins
    On their knees.

Tiny-footed Chinese maids,
With their raven hair in braids,
Sought you in your quiet shades
    'Neath the boughs;—
Haply, for a thousand years,
You beheld their smiles and tears,
Listened to their hopes and fears,
    And their vows.

Now above her escritoire
In my lady's pink boudoir,
Ever dumbly pining for
      Lost repose,
You sit stolid day by day,
With your cheeks so thin and gray,
Stony eyes, and *retroussé*
      Little nose.

Where the sunlight glinteth o'er
Persian rug and polished floor,
You will frown forevermore
      Grim as hate;
A divinity cast down,
Having neither shrine nor crown,
Once a god, but now a brown
      Paper-weight!

A KERCHIEF.

A FILMY fabric, it is true,
   As soft as down and bright as amber,
Brocaded with gay threads as blue
   As flowers that up my trellis clamber.

Upon one silky side behold,
   Embroidered neat, some blooming roses,
While on the other, flecked with gold,
   A bright-winged butterfly reposes.

And though 't is but a trifle, yet
   A something sweet upon it lingers ;
'T is neither " rose " nor " mignonette,"
   But the faint touch of fairy fingers !

MYRTIS.

In dreams I see her drive her flocks,
  When, up a cloudless sky,
Apollo with his golden locks
  At morn is climbing high.
She sings—and, at the witching sound,
  The little larks, in glee,
Wake all the dewy air around
  In vine-clad Thessaly.

The harebells watch to view her pass,
  Like nuns from out their cells,
And peer at her above the grass
  The hosts of asphodels;
Along her path the thyme is sweet
  Where lags the vagrant bee,
The hours fly not with flagging feet
  In vine-clad Thessaly.

MYRTIS.

She featly waves her crook aloft,
   And, lo! there comes straightway,
Adown the hill and through the croft,
   A youth in kirtle gay.
She puts a willing hand in his—
   A happy swain is he!
Would I might woo a maid like this
   In vine-clad Thessaly!

COMPLETION.

The wind went soughing through the spicy pines
   In tender undertone,
The throstles piped amid the tangled vines,
   And soft the sunbeams shone.

Afar old ocean thundered on the rocks
   With blatant, angry sound,
And Neptune drove his emerald-girdled flocks
   To pearly depths profound.

The oaks stood gnarled and grim like witches gray,
   Erect and trim each fir;
The sweet veronica fringed the winding way,
   Pale-hued as lavender.

Like flickering torches through the leafage green
   The orioles fluttered by,

And from the thickets where they lurked unseen
  Was heard the cuckoo's cry.

And yet there seemed a something wanting there
  To make all nature smile,—
When, lo! sweet Clarice, like an oread fair,
  Came down the forest aisle!

THEFT.

I WONDER—just a tiny bit,
As I see Mabel thoughtful sit
    Beside the table,
What she would do, the merry Miss,
If I should steal from her a kiss.
To me it would be perfect bliss,
    But what to Mabel?

Her ear is pink as mother-pearl,
And from her net one golden curl
    Is straying vagrant.
Her silken lashes curve adown
And veil her eyes of bonnie brown;
The perfume from her dainty gown
    Is faintly fragrant.

How easy round her chair to slip,
And press her tempting ruby lip!

THEFT.

    Yet, would I rue it?
What is that saying apt though old?—
A winning knight must needs be bold!—
Then merry Mabel could but scold,—
    I think I'll *do* it!

MOORISH LOVE-SONG.

I think but of thee when with ruby and rose
The sun on the mountains has tinted the snows,
And wakened thine eyes from their dreamy repose.

I think but of thee when the fountains plash sweet
And cool in the noontide amid the still heat,
Like the soft music made by thy two tiny feet.

I think but of thee when the daylight grows pale
On valley and vineyard, on garden and vale,
When warbles so sadly the lorn nightingale.

I think but of thee when the moonbeams outshine
And kiss so divinely each temple and shrine,
And play 'mid the boughs of the citron and pine.

In daylight or darkness, on land or on sea,
In green-girt Granada or far Araby,
My darling, my Zara, I think but of thee!

A BIT OF LACE.

As light as dancing thistle-down,
    This snowy web I gently handle;
It once moved at a maiden's frown
    As now at flicker of the candle.

I know not in what ancient land
    The loom whereon 't was wove of olden,
I cannot tell what slender hand
    First fastened it 'neath ringlets golden.

Perchance some damosel of France
    Once wore it in her boudoir idle,
Mayhap some donna at a dance—
    Why not some beauty at a bridal?

You ask the charm in dainty white,
    As spotless as the lily's chalice?
The bit of lace was worn last night
    Upon the neck of maiden Alice!

"MOTHER HUBBARD."

I take my lyre adown
To praise your pretty gown—
    Your " Mother Hubbard."
You ask me whence the name—
I fancy from that dame
    Of dog and cupboard.

Its hue is scarlet bright,
'T is frilled with laces white,
    Its folds are flowing.
In sooth, 't is sweet to see
You clad so daintily,
    Your cheeks a-glowing.

Methinks 't is quite in taste
The gown should have no waist—
    " You 've said enough, sir !"

MOTHER HUBBARD.

Just one word more—for I
Might find it, on the sly—
 "And get a cuff, sir!"

Ah! pardon me, I pray,
For what I could but say
 Of gown so dainty.
And then a bard, you know,
Should have some rights, and so,
 Why, Bella, may n't he?

TERESA IN THE GARDEN.

Down the garden pathway singing,
   Comes a lithesome form I know ;
Fleet bright butterflies are winging
   To and fro
     On the hillsides where the ox-eyed daisies grow.

Round her flutter thrush and sparrow,
   Warbling joyous, unafraid,
And sly Cupid with his arrow
   'Neath the shade
     Of the rose-tree lurks to greet the laughing maid.

Should he find her there, the charmer,
   With his bended bow and dart,
Pierce the never-shattered armor
   Round her heart,
     Evermore my tongue would bless his subtle art.

TERESA IN THE GARDEN.

See ! she wanders where the roses,
    Jealous, hide her from my view ;
Now an opening fair discloses
    The soft hue
    Of her flitting fleecy garments, skyey blue.

Ah, she pauses ! but 't is only
    By a rose-tree climbing high,
There to pluck a blossom lonely.
    Is he by ?
    Is the love-compelling goddess' son a-nigh ?

Who can tell ? for on she strayeth
    Toward an arbor cool and green,
Where a plashing fountain playeth,
    Soft, serene,
    And beyond in golden wheat-fields reapers glean.

Here amid the vines entwining
    Sits she as the moments pass,
While I gaze with sad repining

At the mass
Of the shining clouds, sun-smit like burnished brass.

Still I wait, my soul a-quiver,
    Till she comes—ah, fate be kind!—
To my heart a joyous giver,
    Where enshrined
    Love will hide beyond the power of ill to find;

Or as calm and cold and stately
    As a statue, marble-born,
Passing with white face sedately,
    Not in scorn,
    Yet to show me how my hopes are all forlorn.

Now the hanging vines are parted
    And I see her draw a-near.
Will she leave me broken-hearted?
    Vanish, Fear!
    In thine eyes I read my answer, thou most dear!

LYRICS AND LAYS.

FORT MARION.

(ST. AUGUSTINE.)

OLD fort, within thy crumbling tower
I stand at this mid-morning hour;
   The sun is hot and high;
Upon the sand-white beach it burns,
While gulls and snowy-breasted terns
   Flit swift athwart the sky.

Along the bay that gleams like wine
I see the shallops toss the brine
   From off their cleaving bows;
And just beyond the island's verge,
With shining sea-weed from the surge
   The Tritons wreathe their brows.

Behind, the old cathedral spire,
Whereon the sunbeams scatter fire,

O'erlooks the sleepy town,
The slave-mart in the shady square,
The sea-wall long and white and bare,
  The houses quaint and brown.

I hear no sound, for silence sways
My soul, and thoughts of by-gone days
  Within my mind arise—
Days when along these bastions wide
The Spaniards stalked with measured stride,
  And dreamed of Cadiz skies.

Then in the moat the lilies white
Brought visions fair of dead delight,
  And eyes that shone like stars;
But now below rank grasses wave,
Perchance o'er many a nameless grave,
  And hide the deadly scars.

Within the dungeons all is still;
The bats and swallows swarm at will
  The guard-room dim and cold;

The cannon-balls lie grim and stark,
Half-hid by vines and mosses dark,
   And crusted thick with mould.

The massive barbacan no more
Beholds the warder pace its floor,
   And swing his clanging keys;
Beneath its vaulted roof the swain
The old, old story tells again,
   And not a trooper sees.

Love hath slipped in between the bars
And driven forth insatiate Mars,
   And reared his altar fair.
Old fortress, thine a happy fate,
For War hath gone from out thy gate,
   And Peace reposeth there.

THE HYMN OF THE PINE.

A SOMBRE sentinel I stand
   Upon the mountain high;
Below my feet outspreads the land,
   Above my head, the sky.

I watch the seasons come and go,
   I see the flowers uplift
Their tender heads beside the snow
   That lies in lingering drift.

I bare my brow to summer's sun
   That parches meadows green,
And dries the rivulets that run
   Like silver threads between.

I joy in autumn gales that bear
   Sweet scents, in crimson morn,

From gardens and from vineyards fair,
    And fields of sickled corn.

I brave the blasts that sting and slay,
    And laugh though loud they roar,
From dawning until dying day,
    Like hounds about my door.

I mark the years like surges roll
    Along the starry skies,
Beyond whose dark cerulean scroll
    Men rear their paradise.

I praise no monarch's puny power
    That on the earth has trod,
But raise my deep voice hour by hour
    In anthems unto God.

ON A BUST OF ANTINOUS.

Upon your beauteous face of sculptured glory,
    A heritage that time should ne'er destroy,
I read your mournful and pathetic story,
        O blithe Bithynian boy.

How through your woodlands green and meadows bloomy
    You roamed at will in glad and childish days,
And dreamed that naught within the world was gloomy,
        And gave the great Gods praise.

Knelt, with your soft cheeks glowing, to Apollo,
    Hung garlands fair where Venus was enshrined,
Heard dryads' voices in the tree trunks hollow,
        Fauns' in the whispering wind.

ON A BUST OF ANTINOUS.

How the proud Cæsar came and you departed,
    Beholding nevermore your happy home,
But following him, capricious, myriad-hearted,
    Unto all-conquering Rome.

How by your truthful artless ways and tender,
    You won the imperious monarch's changeful love ;
How in your soul, his jeers did slow engender
    Distrust of Gods above.

How by the Tiber, in the sunlight golden,
    While round you frowned the Olympians, now disowned,
You pondered long o'er many a volume olden
    Of creeds long since dethroned.

How, when encamped on fiery sands Egyptian,
    You, seeking truth beneath their God's dark brows,
Were lured to death by some priest-wrought inscription,
    Believing in their vows.

I seem to see, as graven with a stylus,
  The last sad scene, your pitiful despair,
The slow and sombre flow of dismal Nilus,—
  To hear your parting prayer.

Thus in the loyal hope of death forefending
  From his proud heart who gave so little joy,
You brought your life to sacrificial ending,
  O blithe Bithynian boy!

TO A MOCKING-BIRD.

You waken me at early morn
    With your sweet notes and trills,
Ere yet Apollo's rays adorn
    With gold the wood-capped hills,
Or touch the tassel-waving corn,
    Or silver all the rills.

You pipe, you sing, your voice you tune
    Through every fleeting hour,
With you the days are always June,
    The meads always in flower ;
You carol at the sheeny moon
    From your embalméd bower.

Just now your song methinks I heard
    The robin redbreast sing,
And now 't is like that timid bird,
    The thrush of early spring,

And now as though the silence stirred
   With orioles twittering.

The bobolink you mimic sly,
   The thievish catbird call,
You speak the swallow, darting by,
   The wren within the wall,
The lark uprising to the sky
   With holy madrigal.

Your life is like your welling song,
   A still enduring flow
Of gladness, where the joys that throng
   Are darkened ne'er by woe;
Then sing, blithe bird, sing full and strong,
   We bless you, singing so!

SAPPHO.

WITHIN the sea-girt Lesbian land
   To-day there burns no altar fire,
Forgotten is the magic hand
   That once so sweetly swept the lyre.

And thou, O Mitylene, great
   In days when Greece was giant-strong,
Art fallen from thine high estate,
   Though birthplace of a queen of song.

The clear waves shimmer in the sun
   As when of old she walked thy shores,
And saw the galleys, one by one,
   Sweep by, with banks of shining oars;

Saw Persians, with their fabrics fine,
   In gay and thickly-thronged bazaars,

And heard the gallants at their wine
    When night had sown the sky with stars.

All knew her then and gave her praise:
    For her was honor, glory, fame—
And poets, crowned with Delphic bays,
    To her o'er wide Ægean came.

But calumny, that scorpion base,
    Hath blackened long her honor rare;
And all mankind, ay! every race,
    Yet scorns the name that once was fair.

Why should she bear another's guilt
    Whose life was full of love and pure?
Would to her dust there might be built
    A cenotaph that should endure!

Somewhere she lies in perfect peace,
    Unmindful of this ruthless wrong:
Then let the tongues of slander cease,
    And praise be hers, defamed so long!

AN AUTUMN SCENE.

The dead leaves fall like noiseless rain,
    The air is calm and warm and sweet;
Upon the woodland and the plain
    The ghost of Summer rests her feet.

A languid fountain sends its spray
    Into a basin, green with moss;
Slim water-spiders pass in play
    Where flickering sunbeams dance across.

A spirit broods o'er all unseen,
    And soon will chill with icy breath.
The peace, so restful and serene,
    Is but the calm that comes with death.

MORNING ON THE MOUNTAINS.

(SIERRA MADRE.)

The leaden clouds in cumbrous masses
    Gloom high above the mountain wall,
And overhang the rocky passes
    Where tinkling ice-born streamlets fall.

Athwart the east, through mist-banks riven,
    The sun hurls down his golden shafts,
And from the snowy summits driven,
    Come morning's keen inspiring draughts.

Along the silence-stricken valley
    Long lagging trains of *burros* wind,
Their lazy Mexique drivers dally
    Amid the mesquite far behind.

Across the wakening dome of heaven
    The ravens wheel with startling yell;

The linnet lifts her simple steven
   Within the thorny chaparral.

The lofty peaks whose fleecy shoulders
   Are clad with juniper and pine,
And giant lichen-crusted bowlders,
   Along the bright horizon shine.

And here where brambles intermingle,
   A cactus, like a slender tower,
Lifts a slim stalk whereon a single
   Bright bud is bursting into flower.

An awful grandeur, mystic, holy,
   Fills all this sparkling upper air,
And bows the spirit to a lowly
   And reverent mood that ends in prayer.

And yet a sense of desolation
   Pervades these heights where few have trod,
For not a human habitation
   Stands where the mountains look to God.

A FAIR NOVICE.

Sweet maid, thy face is fair as one may see
   Among Madonnas of the masters old ;
Yet sad thou art as tearful Niobe,
    Carved from the heart of Parian marble cold
    By one who slumbers now 'neath Attic mold ;
Thy lips were framed for lover's whispered "yes,"
    To sing in bower where burns the marigold
And breezes breathe no sigh of bitterness.

I see thee pace adown the garden way
    From my lone window 'bove the convent wall,
The purple blossoms of the dying May
    Seem fain to kiss thy feet so slender-small ;
    Of flowers thou art the fairest flower of all,
Unmeet to bloom within a prison bower,
    Where stony Silence holds the heart in thrall,
And Penance marks with pallid hands the hour.

Ah! could I read thy secret from thine eyes,
    What mournful sorrow were it mine to know?
Was life once sunny as the bright June skies
    Ere cold Death winged the dart that laid love low?
    Didst thou, heart-weary, to the cloister go,
And kneeling there before the sacred shrine,
    Don those gray garments that bespeak thy woe,
And consecrate thy life to things divine?

Does longing ne'er rekindle in thy breast
    For shady lanes and quiet greenwood ways,
When thou beholdest, in their verdure dressed,
    The stirring branches giving leafy praise
    Unto the Shaper of the nights and days,
When, from thy casement in the amber morn,
    Thou hearest anthems that the glad birds raise
'Mong scented blossoms on the pinky thorn?

Alas! that life for thee is void of joy,
    Unless, perchance, joy springs from kindly deed;
Pale Pain and Grief have wrought a dark alloy
    And in thy soul have sown the bitter seed.

Ah! would that one might succor thee in need,
That Eros' torch might fire thy heart again,
  Which evermore from Sorrow's shafts must bleed,
A throne for love where love can never reign!

AMID THE MARSHES.

(AT RYE.)

I HEAR the loud booming
  Of surf on the shore,
Afar I see looming
  The head of the Boar,
And there out to seaward
  The dark islands lie,
With ships to the leeward,
  White specks on the sky.

Gray-green are the bowlders
  That lie on the land,
Uplifting rough shoulders
  High over the sand;
The wide marsh outreaches
  With sunlight aglow,

To where on the beaches
    The foam is like snow.

The dark rushes quiver,
    Astir in the breeze,
The flags are a-shiver
    Like leaves on the trees;
And through the thick grasses
    A soft zephyr creeps,
That moves, as it passes,
    The willow that weeps.

The blackbirds are nesting
    Where cat-tails are tall,
The plovers are resting
    To hear their mates call,
The swallows go winging
    O'er waters that dream,
The robins are singing
    A-nigh the clear stream.

I catch, seaward blowing,
    The spice of the pine,

And scent the inflowing
    Salt smell of the brine ;
I see the pools darkle
    Where shadow is cast,
And watch the waves sparkle
    Where ripples slip past.

Tall, crowning yon island
    Of moss-bank and sod,
Bright flower of the dry land,
    The gay golden-rod,
With pennons outstreaming,
    Stands fair to behold,
Beneath the broad-beaming,
    Round day-orb of gold.

O marshes that sever
    The sea and the land,
In glad summer ever
    You beauteous stand !
Yet soon, as in slaughter,
    The north wind will roar

Adown the dark water
  From stark Labrador;

Wan ice will encumber
  Your rushes and reeds,
Black storms without number
  Will loosen their steeds,
The snows will emboss thee,
  And loud, like the flail,
Along and across thee
  Will clatter the hail.

The sun that shone o'er thee
  No longer will shine,
The birds that adore thee
  No more will be thine,
Around, like a Gorgon,
  With pitiless breath,
The ocean's deep organ
  Will trumpet of death.

Will this be eternal
  And changeless? Ah! no—

The south breezes vernal
  Will soften the snow,
Again will the swallow
  With love-songs beguile,
Again will Apollo
  Benignantly smile.

Wave on then, O rushes,
  Sing on then, O bird—
The winter but hushes
  Thy song without word,
For sweeter and clearer
  Again 'twill up-soar,
And seem the far dearer,
  And charm but the more!

THE CROCUS.

We see thy sweet face, when, within the valleys,
   Loud roar the swollen rills,
While yet the storm-wind ominously dallies
   Around the snow-crowned hills.

E'en as a bright-winged fairy thou upspringest
   From out the wizened earth,
And dreams of pleasure unalloyed thou bringest
   With thine auspicious birth.

Thou markest the return of faun and satyr
   That dance down ferny dells,
Whose nimble footsteps we hear faintly patter
   Among the wild harebells.

Thou art as welcome as a maiden bearing
   Some cool, delicious balm

To one who long through waste lands hath been far-
   ing,
   In search of sheltering palm.

Few are the hearts, be they or proud or lowly,
   Beneath heaven's azure sea,
That are not touched with an emotion holy,
   At sight, dear flower, of thee!

A SPRIG OF HEATHER.

(NANTUCKET.)

WANDERER from foreign leas,
Girt around by stormy seas,
Where thy blue bells brave the breeze
    In wild weather,
Why didst choose this lonely isle
In our land of sun and smile
For thy home this weary while,
    Scottish heather?

Many a fairer isle there is,
Many a brighter one than this,
If to dwell thou wouldst not miss
    On an island;
Sunnier slopes thou mightest find,
More befitting to thy kind,

Like, if thou hadst in mind,
>>Thine own Highland.

Now thou canst not aid and cheer
Mourning hearts that shed the tear,
Far from home and kindred dear,
>>O'er the ocean !
Many, could they see thy crest,
Bonnie little flower so blest,
Would no more feel in the breast
>>Sad emotion.

But it is thy choice, not ours,—
We have other sweeter flowers,
Gayer far, to deck our bowers,
>>Fair for seeing ;—
Yet somehow we know thou art
Dearer, closer to the heart,
And to some a very part
>>Of their being.

A SONG FOR NOVEMBER.

WIDE o'er the wold,
Through field and fold,
The wind moans cold,
And sighs in sadness;
The dreamy days
Have gone their ways,
Like flitting fays
That dance in gladness.

Dead are the leaves
And stored the sheaves,
Lone are the eaves
Where sang the swallow;
In robes of black
The cloudy wrack
Obscures the track
Where shone Apollo.

A SONG FOR NOVEMBER.

  No more the wain
  From fertile plain
  Doth bear the grain
Of golden reaping;
  The meads are sere,
  The woods are drear,
  And dead, the year
Will soon be sleeping.

  Not now, alas!
  In bending grass,
  A merry mass
The thrush is trilling;
  The lark no more
  Doth sing and soar;
  On southern shore
The wren is billing.

  No blossoms bright
  Of red and white
  Set sweet delight
Of fragrance floating;

A SONG FOR NOVEMBER.

  All that was fair
  Is bleak and bare;
  The gardens wear
A russet coating.

  At dreary dawn
  On lea and lawn,
  Where, in days gone,
Was gay adorning,
  No Jacqueminot
  Doth bud and blow,
  Or, face aglow,
Turn east at morning.

  The wary sprite,
  At noon of night,
  In wan moonlight
Doth shake and shiver;
  The nymphs have fled
  And Pan is dead;
  No boatmen thread
The narrow river.

But why repine,
O heart of mine?
Joy still is thine,
Though days grow colder;
And snows will bring,
In fragrant spring,
Fresh blossoming
From flowers that molder!

REVERIE.

At darkling night, when day has flown,
    And lisping raindrops patter low,
    When, like sere harbingers of snow,
Across the lawn dead leaves are blown,
Then would I lie, and dream alone,
    Upon a couch, in languorous ease,
Of sunny lands and bliss unknown
    Beyond the sapphire seas.

There, like the sunlight-dancing mote,
    Would I, to emerald shores conveyed,
    Adown some river's dim arcade
Through peerless water-lilies float;
    And hear the whispering leaves breathe out
Their tender touching melodies,
And see, beneath the olive trees,
    The lovers stroll about.

Or through a city old and drear
    At radiant noontide would I go,
    In ruffled lace and tall chapeau,
Like gay and gallant cavalier,
    Meeting, perchance, Boccaccio,
    By lovely Arno's songful flow,
Commingling with the throng to hear
    Their jests or tales of woe.

But dearer far at eve to stroll
Along thy winding ways, Stamboul,
    And catch above some gay bazaar
The liquid glance of Eastern eyes,
And in the blue of Eastern skies
    Behold the paling crescent shine,
And hear sweet Safie's voice afar,
    Then feel her hand in mine.

NIGHT ON THE OCHLAWAHA.

THE air was full of vague alarms,
    And from the shuddering cypress trees
That threw abroad their giant arms,
    Strange sounds stole down the breeze.

The river, like a serpent slow,
    Wound through the forest, fold on fold,
And caught the lambent torch's glow
    In glints of ruddy gold.

Like somber harbingers of ill,
    The livid mosses waved in air;
While water monsters, stark and still,
    Slept in each reedy lair.

A dusky wide-winged bird swept by
    And silent, vanished, like a ghost

That hurrieth onward drearily
  To join some spirit host.

A dismal sound our senses smote,—
  A moment,—like a dream 't was gone ;
We thought of Charon's grim black boat
  On gloomy Acheron !

FAREWELL AND HAIL.

FAREWELL to ceaseless snowing,
   And winter garbed in gray !
Too long his chains have bound us,
We 'll fling them from around us,
And gleeful hail his going
   With ringing roundelay :
Farewell to ceaseless snowing,
   And winter garbed in gray !

Away with pallid pining
   And sorrowing that 's vain !
Soon skies will smile above us,
And tender lilies love us,
And warmer suns be shining
   Upon the amber grain ;
Away with pallid pining
   And sorrowing that 's vain !

We 'll dream that pain is over,
   And grief that wastes and wears ;
We 'll roam the fields with Dian,
Or hunt with bold Orion,
Or play the reckless rover
   Where quivered Cupid fares ;
We 'll dream that pain is over,
   And grief that wastes and wears !

We 'll lie amid the rushes
   And tune a pipe with Pan ;
We 'll sport with fays and fairies,
Whose green-embowered lair is
Where thicket-loving thrushes
   Make melody for man ;
We 'll lie amid the rushes
   And tune a pipe with Pan !

RETROSPECTION.

To-night there's a hush 'mong the roses,
    The casement wide open is thrown,
A glimmer of starlight discloses
    Pale virginal lilies full-blown;
I breathe the sweet cool air inflowing
    From meadows besprent with the dew
Where the maidenly daisies are growing,
    And think, my old comrade, of you.

I hear that you're fêted and lauded,
    That the world knows your face and your name,
That your speeches are loudly applauded,
    That you're climbing the ladder of fame;
Yet in spite of it all I still wonder
    If you're heart-free and happy as when
Like brothers we twain wandered under
    The sycamores shading the glen.

RETROSPECTION.

How well I recall all the longing
    You used to confide in those days,
And the visions that ever came thronging
    Your brain, of the world and its ways!
How blissful it was to go drifting
    Adown the calm river at morn,
Aurora her bright brow uplifting,
    And Dian a-winding her horn!

How we loved to recline on the grasses,
    When afternoon breezes were cool,
And gaze at the mountainous masses
    Of clouds in the depths of the pool!
How at twilight we lingered to listen
    To the low vesper song of the birds,
Till we saw the bright fireflies out-glisten
    Among the late-pasturing herds!

Ah, those days are like images graven
    Upon some dark room of my brain!
Now and then, in that dim-lighted haven,
    I joyfully see them again;

And I turn from the wrangle and quarrel,
    From the strife for success and renown,
To think of the bay-leaf and laurel
    And dream I have won me a crown.

DECEMBER.

The hills look gaunt in russet garb:
    Against the sky the leafless woods
    Are dark, and in their solitudes
The chill wind pierces like a barb.

The naked branches grimly clutch
    The sullen clouds that threaten snow,
    And near the streamlet's icy flow
An old man rests upon his crutch.

A comrade of the dying year,
    Upon his wrinkled brow sits Age:
    And yet he hath for heritage
A brighter life, so spare your tear!

THEOCRITUS.

Great bard whose liquid lines did first awaken
  Within my heart a deathless love of song,
O'er meads by thee for many a year forsaken
  Once more I see thee blithely pass along.

Within thy hand the stout staff of a shepherd,
  Across thy shoulders, like a mantle thrown,
The tawny skin of some light-footed leopard
  That by a beech bole gave its dying moan.

And following thy steps with merry paces
  A throng of lads and lasses laughing free,
Joyful to feel the west wind fan their faces,
  Fresh from the billows of the tossing sea.

I watch thee pause beneath an oak tree gnarly,
  Thy eager listeners gathering gayly round,

And bending toward thee like the blades of barley
  That lean to catch the pattering rain-drops' sound.

They hear thee there retell in flowing measure,
  As sweet as is the purl of waters cool,
How Jason won the fleece, that priceless treasure,
  And how the nymphs lured Hylas to the pool.

And lulled by all thy golden-worded fancies
  They drowse throughout the glowing afternoon,
Till darkness shivers Phœbus' shining lances
  And softly beams the fair Sicilian moon.

And in the odorous twilight calm and stilly,
  What time the hillside cricket chirps elate,
From out the fields where sways the purple lily
  They gain the stately city's guarded gate.

While through the lone night watches stalks the warder,
  In dreams they sail the shining jasper seas,
And roam with thee the gardens green that border
  Those blissful islands, the Hesperides.

Grand is this power of song that bridgeth over
 　The yawning gulfs of the destroyer Time,
For one may wander like an airy rover
 　Down sleeping ages on the wings of rhyme;

Behold the past outspread with all its wonder,
 　As Moses saw from Nebo's mount of old,
When clouds and darkness had been rent asunder,
 　Afar the peaceful promised land unfold!

IN THE MISSION BURIAL-GROUND.

(SAN GABRIEL.)

I STOOD knee-deep in grasses green ;
   Within the clambering vines the birds
   Seemed uttering pathetic words,
Sweet choristers unseen.

I saw the crosses wan and white,
   The sunken graves, the tender flowers,
   The hillside bright from freshening showers,
The sky ablaze with light ;

The mission gray and grim and old,
   The bells that ever voiceless stand,
   And, far above the level land,
The mountains stern and cold.

I caught the aromatic scent
   Of dying roses on the air,
   And o'er my senses, like a prayer,
There stole a calm content.

HERRICK.

Down Devon's dales returning spring
Brings timid larks that soar and sing,
   And buds on hawthorne hedges;
But there no songs like thine take wing
Of love, and swains a-shepherding,
   And jovial Bacchic pledges.

As merry are thy laughing lays
As his who gained Hipparchus' praise,
   And hymned the vine-god's glories;
As his of glad Sicilian days,
Or his who won Augustan bays
   By honey-sweet *amores*.

What loves were thine! First, Julia fair,
Enthroned in graces far more rare
   Than Grecian Autonöe;
Dianame, Electra share

Thy rich regard, and thee in snare
   Had Sylvia gay, and Chloe.

Thine age was one of mighty men !
Dame Wit with Wisdom married then.
   As later time confesses.
Will Shakspere, Bacon, "rare old Ben "—
Can such a reign be known again
   As was the good Queen Bess's ?

We, like thy friends of pastoral creed,
In honor to thy blithesome reed
   Would raise the ivied thyrses ;
Thy prophecy proves true indeed,
Of praise thou hast a worthy meed,
   Thy "pillar" still thy verses !

AN AUGUST NOON.

Day's glowing orb with stifling heat
    Flames red within a brazen sky;
Upon the vacant, soundless street
    The maple's lifeless shadows lie.

The bell in swallow-swarming arch
    Has tolled the parching noontide hour;
Gray Time on his fleet-footed march
    Notes not the season, sun nor shower.

The hush is deep where leaves astir
    Were murmuring in the morning cool,
The blackbird dozes in the fir,
    The marsh-bird by the rushy pool.

About the stagnant fountain's edge
    Flit dragon-flies with gauzy wing,

AN AUGUST NOON.

The thrush sits silent in the hedge,
   In languor he forgets to sing.

Gay butterflies dance to and fro,
   Blithe mates of amber, red and blue;
On such still noons long, long ago
   Sped by Diana and her crew;

Sped by the goddess with her maids
   To seek some lonely woodland mere,
And there, beneath the grateful shades,
   Sport in the water calm and clear.

Pan piped beside the gurgling brook,
   And charmed the rustics, pasture-bound,—
The shepherd boy with vine-clad crook
   Stood breathless at the entrancing sound.

Such simple pastoral days have fled
   With phantoms of forgotten years,
Though bards then crowned and garlanded
   Sang songs that echo in our ears;

Bucolic strains, in measures meet,
    Of thymy mead and asphodel,
And plaintive love-songs, softly sweet,
    Of Cynthia and Philomel.

We love those glad good days of old,
    When men not yet were over-wise,
And sought in something else than gold
    To find an " earthly Paradise."

Yet who would wish it back once more,
    The happy past of deathless rhyme ?
The present, from our restless shore,
    Calls out : " To-day is golden time ! "

A LILY OF THE VALLEY.

(Blooming in winter.)

O TENDEREST blossom of the year,
   In winter's dreary watches born,
Thou bringest to us thoughts of cheer
   In days forlorn.

Not now we heed the deep-voiced knells
   Of seried storm-winds, raging bold,
But gazing on thy spotless bells,
   Forget the cold.

Forget that feathery drifts are high
   Within the garden's bowery close,
That now no wooing sunlit sky
   Smiles on the rose.

But dream that zephyrs move the grass
   Along the cricket-peopled hill,

And stir the ripples as they pass
  Above the rill;

That wood-wrens twitter in the hush
  Of tangled copses at mid-noon,
That blackbirds haunt the river rush,
  That now 't is June.

And in the dewy twilight's dusk,
  Where apple branches intertwine,
Amid the heavy scent of musk,
  Like spicèd wine,

Again we see a maiden band
  As merry as the laughing Hours,
Each deftly weaving in her hand
  A wreath of flowers;

A wreath wherein thy slender stems
  And tender cuplets, snowy pale,
Shame all the gayer blossom-gems
  That deck the dale.

The song the damsels sang that eve
  From memory's mystic isles out-blown,

Dies like a happy dream, to leave
    The vision flown.

And thee alone we now behold,
    O fairest of all flowerets born,
A guerdon to the heart a-cold,
    In days forlorn!

THE SAILING OF THE SEA GULL.
1820.

Would you hear a sailor's story, land-blown from
    the tossing seas,
  From Atlantic-girt Nantucket and the windmill
    on its crown,
Told me by a hardy seaman, by a swarthy Portu-
    guese,
  Of the sailing of the Sea Gull from the quaint
    old island town?

'T was a morning mild and merry with the balmy
    breath of spring,
  When the apple bloom and cherry whitened
    every fragrant bough,
And the hoarse-voiced old town-crier, calling loudly,
    sought to bring
  All the young folk and the old folk to the ship of
    golden prow.

THE SAILING OF THE SEA GULL.

For the Sea Gull had upon her a strange figure-
    head of gold,
  Of a sea bird letting sun her spreading pinions,
    wondrous wide,
Which the captain found when hidden in a Spanish
    pirate's hold
  On a lovely coral island, in the Gulf Stream's
    tropic tide.

Many a happy youth and maiden hurried down-
    ward to the quay,
  Where the stately ship lay laden with the strength
    of all the isle,
With those fearless ocean-rovers who had scoured
    the trackless sea
  From the icy Bay of Baffin to Fuego's rocky
    pile.

Who had seen the fire-capped summit of the peak
    of Teneriffe
  Loom afar amid the cloudland when the summer
    day was calm,

Who had braved the savage Malays, boarding from
    the proa and skiff,
  When they idly lay at anchor off the shores of
    pearl and palm.

Vows were soft and sadly spoken, for young, tender hearts were there,
  Hearts yet hopeful and unbroken by the sorrow-teeming years,
Loving kisses, shyly given by the maidens coy and fair,
  Sparkling eyes, the hue of heaven, dimmed with sad, foreboding tears.

And with shouts that made the morning echo, proudly from the shore
  Swung the Sea Gull, like a petrel, poising, ere it fly afar;
Then the west wind caught her canvas and she leaped the waters o'er,
  Passed the nightly-flaring beacon and the sunken harbor bar.

Many watched her as she faded in the blue horizon line,
  With their tearful eyelids shaded by the trembling lily hand,
Till at last they saw no vessel on the wide-extending brine—
  Saw naught save the endless ocean and the white, shell-dotted sand.

Then they wended slowly homeward, but to watch and wait in vain ;
  While the Sea Gull, ever foam-ward, down the wild Atlantic drove,
Till the lookout shouted, "Land ho!" as they sailed the Spanish Main,
  And they anchored near an island in a cliff-encircled cove.

Thence, when they had drawn the nectar from the purling, pebbly brook,
  And had waited till the ocean ruffled gently in the breeze,

Slowly drawing out to seaward, still a southern course they took,
  Till, a faint speck far to leeward, lay the emerald Caribees.

Fair the gales that followed after; veering Fortune seemed to smile.
  Went the balmy days in laughter ere they reached the stormy Horn.
Then the gentle-browed Pacific their long watches did beguile,
  And they hailed her face with gladness on a crimson-cheekèd morn.

Soon they found the islands bloomy and the waters clear and deep,
  Where, from ocean hollows gloomy, yet unpierced by restless man,
Come the throngs of mighty monsters there to sport with plunge and leap,
  And the gallant Sea Gull conquered many a huge leviathan.

Then with hearts that gayly bounded, from those crystal seas they bore,
   Once again they safely rounded the dark sentinel that frowns
Back the harsh and fierce Antarctic from the rocky southern shore,
   Where it beats in noisy tumult on its barren, icy bounds.

But the favoring winds no longer gently filled the fluttering sails,
   For grim Boreas, waxing stronger, put fair Zephyrus to flight,
And then howling down the highways of the ocean with his gales,
   Brought despair from out the by-ways of the sullen-visaged Night.

Many a day they knew not whither, swift before the blast they flew,
   Till no more the stately Sea Gull was her dauntless captain's boast;

But at last the storm clouds lifted and they saw the shining blue,
    And afar the hazy outline of the torrid Afric coast.

When the next night's dusk had deepened, calm came o'er the fretted sea,
    Silver-robed, serene Selene showed her glowing disk afar ;
Every scudding cloud had vanished, and the orbèd arch was free,
    Regal now, though lately banished, radiant shone each sovereign star.

And the Sea Gull swiftly speeding, all her snowy canvas spread,
    Darted onward, no one heeding that the dread Fates hovered near ;
Few the lookouts, as the sailors, each one in his hammock bed,
    Worn and weary, slumbered deeply, for the night was wondrous clear.

Suddenly, at hailing distance, white a monstrous ship up-loomed,
    Bearing down without resistance straight across the Sea Gull's track.
None beheld the awful danger, and the hapless men were doomed,—
    Doomed, alas! to sink unaided to the caverns cold and black.

Swift the mighty crash and fatal, then reigned silence as before,
    For the proud but stricken vessel had been almost riven in twain;
In a moment the dark waters closed above her, and no more
    Sailed the Sea Gull like a swallow o'er the billows of the main.

Such the sad old voyager's story from the wild, remorseless seas,
    As I heard it in the hoary windmill on Nantucket's crown;

He alone brought back the tidings, he, the swarthy Portuguese,
How the bravest of the island and her stanchest ship went down.

BALLADES, ETC.

BALLADE TO VILLON.

WHERE, prithee, are thy comrades bold,
   With ruffle, flounce and furbelow,
Who, in the merry days of old,
   Made light of all but red wine's flow?
   Where now are cavalier and beau
Who joyed with thee in that bright clime?
   Ah! dust to dust!—and none may know—
Alas! for the fleet wings of Time!

Where now are they whom gleaming gold
   Led on to many a bandit blow,
Who roamed with thee the widening wold
   And vine-clad hills, and shared thy woe?
   Where they, who, in the sunset glow,
With thee heard Paris' sweet bells chime?
   Ah! they are gone!—and still men go—
Alas! for the fleet wings of Time!

And where are they, those maids untold,
   Thy lighter loves, each one thy foe?
They too are now but loathsome mold,
   With earth above and earth below.
   And she who won, aside to throw
Thy love, the promise of thy prime,
   Doth any seek her name?—ah! no—
Alas! for the fleet wings of Time!

ENVOY.

Poet of ballade and rondeau,
   Prince of the tripping, laughing rhyme,
Thy name alone hath 'scaped the snow;
   Alas! for the fleet wings of Time!

BALLADE OF DEAD POETS.

THEOCRITUS, who bore
  The lyre where sleek herds graze
On the Sicilian shore,
  (There yet the shepherd strays)—
  And Horace, crowned with bays,
Who dwelt by Tiber's flow,
  Sleep through the silent days—
For God will have it so!

The bard, whose requiem o'er
  And o'er the sad sea plays,
Who sang of classic lore,
  Of Mab, the queen of fays—
  And Keats, fair Adonais,
The child of song and woe,
  No longer thread life's maze—
For God will have it so!

Your voices, sweet of yore
    With honied word and phrase,
Are heard by men no more,
    They list to other lays—
    New poets now have praise,
But all in turn must go
    To follow in your ways—
For God will have it so!

ENVOY.

Poets, the thrones ye raise
    Are not a "fleeting show";
Fame lives, though dust decays—
    For God will have it so!

BALLADE FOR A WEDDING.

May fair Aurora gayly gild
   Mead, mountain, moor and main,
May all the crystal rills be filled
   And woo the greening plain,
   May apple-blossoms fall like rain
And buds blush on the thorn—
   May Clotho wind a golden skein
Upon thy wedding morn !

Among the mating birds that build
   'Mid boughs that sway like grain,
May not one happy note be stilled
   And not one song be vain,
   But soothe the hearts that pine in pain
And brighten those forlorn ;
   May Grief lie like a foeman slain
Upon thy wedding morn !

May some great poet-soul be thrilled
    To passion's lofty strain ;
May jewels wrought by craftsmen skilled—
    Fit gems for Dian's fane—
    And fabrics fine of purple stain
That princely looms adorn,
    As gifts before thy feet be lain
Upon thy wedding morn !

ENVOY.

Sweet lady, may thy joy ne'er wane,
    Thy love ne'er turn to scorn !
May Mirth lead in her tripping train
    Upon thy wedding morn !

BALLADE OF THE BARD.

THOUGH through the cloudy ranks of morn
    The Sun-god sends no golden ray,
Though swift along the air are borne
    The feathery shafts that none may stay,
    Though wrathful storm-blasts pangless slay,
And wan the patient plodder rues
    His lonely lot each dragging day—
He's gay who courts the merry muse!

When down the fields the tender corn
    Upsprings, and sees blue skies in May,
When budding blooms the boughs adorn,
    And flowers bespangle sprig and spray,
    When torrid summer's regnant sway
Has dimmed the foliage's fairest hues,
    And bronzèd reapers house the hay—
He's gay who courts the merry muse!

And when the hollow harvest horn
    O'erflows with autumn's rich display,
When high, with goodly grain, new-shorn,
    Is piled each lofty granary,
    When, like dark moons amid the gray
Of cornfields, where the red ear woos,
    The pumpkins lie in long array—
He's gay who courts the merry muse!

ENVOY.

Prince, e'en though Fortune go astray,
    And lost is wealth's bright-shining cruse,
Though dark and drear the weary way—
    He's gay who courts the merry muse!

THE PRAYER OF DRYOPE.

(RONDEAU REDOUBLÉ.)

O GODDESS sweet give ear unto my prayer,
    Come with thy doves across the briny sea,
Leave thy tall fanes and thy rose gardens rare,
    From cruel bondage set thy vot'ress free!

Ah! how my heart would joy again to be
    Like chirming bird that cleaves the sunny air,
Like wildwood roe that bounds in ecstasy;
    O goddess sweet, give ear unto my prayer!

That I am innocent, hast thou no care,
    Of crime against celestial deity?
Must I the fate of lovely Lotis share?—
    Come with thy doves across the briny sea!

I hear no water's silvern melody,
    And yet the rippling river once was there,

And on its bloomy banks I worshipped thee;—
    Leave thy tall fanes and thy rose gardens rare!

Could I but feel my boy's hands on my hair,
    Could I but kiss my sister Iole,
Then bravely would I cast forth chill despair,
    From cruel bondage set thy vot'ress free!

I, who was once the blithesome Dryope,
    Am now a tree bole, cold and brown and bare;
Pity, I pray, my ceaseless agony,
    Or grant forgetfulness of all things fair,
                  O goddess sweet!

AT PEEP OF DAWN.

(RONDEAU.)

At peep of dawn the daffodil
That slumbers 'neath the grassy hill,
   Greets smilingly, with lifted head,
   The rosy Morn's oncoming tread,
The thrush sings matins by the rill.

The swallows from the ruined mill
Go coursing through the air, and fill
   The sky with songs till then unsaid
                At peep of dawn.

No harbinger of day is still.
With pipe new-tuned and merry trill,
   The lark uprises from her bed
   'Mong grasses wet with dews unshed,
And puts to shame the whip-poor-will
                At peep of dawn.

WHEN SIRIUS SHINES.

(RONDEAU.)

When Sirius shines, a fulgent fire,
And locusts in a drowsy choir
   At noon within the maples drone,
   And pines at nightfall make sad moan
Like waves upon the rocks of Tyre,

Then strike the softly sounding lyre,
And let the soaring song rise higher,
   Or fall to minor monotone
                 When Sirius shines

But should the chiming voices tire,
And thoughts of past and vain desire
   Refill the mind, as doves once flown
   Return to cotes aforetime known,
Let then the soul to heaven aspire,
                 When Sirius shines.

VIS EROTIS.

(RONDEAU.)

Love that holdeth firm in fee
   Many a lord of many a land,
From thy thraldom few would flee,
Wide the wondrous potency
   Of thy heart-enchaining hand.

Since on shining Cyprian sand
Did thy mother, Venus, stand,
   Man and maid have worshipped thee,
               Love.

They that scorn thy slaves to be,
   Oft before thy throne, unmanned,
Grant thy great supremacy ;
   Hear my prayer, O monarch, and
Let my lady smile on me,
               Love.

I HEARD A MAID WITH HER GUITAR.

(RONDEL.)

I HEARD a maid with her guitar
    Who played, like Orpheus, to the wind,
And sent forth rythmic notes afar
    From out an arbor vine-entwined.

She knew the God of love was blind,
    And left her white heart-gates ajar—
I heard a maid with her guitar
    Who played, like Orpheus, to the wind.

But ah! Love's ears are keen as are
    The ears of shy, pool-haunting hind,
And when she closed her bosom's bar
    She found the god was there enshrined;
I heard a maid with her guitar
    Who played, like Orpheus, to the wind.

UPON THE STAIR I SEE MY LADY STAND.

(RONDEL.)

Upon the stair I see my lady stand,
  Her hair is like the gleaming gold of dawn,
  And, like the laughing sunbeam on the lawn,
The radiant smile by which her lips are spanned.

A chiselled marvel seems her slender hand
  What time she waves it ere my steps are gone;
Upon the stair I see my lady stand,
  Her hair is like the gleaming gold of dawn.

Through the green covert that the breeze has fanned
  She fleets as graceful as the flexile fawn;
  She is the star to which my soul is drawn
When shadows drive the daylight from the land.
Upon the stair I see my lady stand,
  Her hair is like the gleaming gold of dawn.

A SNOWFLAKE IN MAY.

(TRIOLET.)

I saw a snowflake in the air
   When smiling May had decked the year,
And then 't was gone, I knew not where,—
I saw a snowflake in the air,
And thought perchance an angel's prayer
   Had fallen from some starry sphere;
I saw a snowflake in the air
   When smiling May had decked the year.

IN THE SULTAN'S GARDEN.

(PANTOUM.)

She oped the portal of the palace,
    She stole into the garden's gloom;
From every spotless snowy chalice
    The lilies breathed a sweet perfume.

She stole into the garden's gloom,
    She thought that no one would discover;
The lilies breathed a sweet perfume,
    She swiftly ran to meet her lover.

She thought that no one would discover,
    But footsteps followed, ever near :
She swiftly ran to meet her lover
    Beside the fountain crystal clear.

But footsteps followed ever near;
    Ah, who is that she sees before her

Beside the fountain crystal clear?
    'T is not her hazel-eyed adorer.

Ah, who is that she sees before her,
    His hand upon his scimitar?
'T is not her hazel-eyed adorer,
    It is her lord of Candahar!

His hand upon his scimitar—
    Alas, what brought such dread disaster!
It is her lord of Candahar,
    The fierce Sultan, her lord and master.

Alas, what brought such dread disaster!
    "Your pretty lover's dead!" he cries—
The fierce Sultan, her lord and master—
    "'Neath yonder tree his body lies."

"Your pretty lover's dead!" he cries—
    (A sudden, ringing voice behind him);
"'Neath yonder tree his body lies—"
    "Die, lying dog! go thou and find him!"

A sudden, ringing voice behind him,
   A deadly blow, a moan of hate,
" Die, lying dog ! go thou and find him !
   Come, love, our steeds are at the gate ! "

A deadly blow, a moan of hate,
   His blood ran red as wine in chalice ;
" Come, love, our steeds are at the gate ! "
   She oped the portal of the palace.

VILLANELLE TO HELEN.

Man's very voice is stilled on Troas' shore,
  Sweet Xanthus and Simois both are mute,
Thus have the gods ordained forevermore !

Springs the rank weed where bloomed the rose before,
  Unplucked on Ida hangs the purple fruit,
Man's very voice is stilled on Troas' shore.

Where heavenly walls towered proud and high of yore,
  Unharmed now strays abroad the savage brute,
Thus have the gods ordained forevermore !

And they, the wronged, that wasting sorrow bore,
  Alas ! their tree hath withered to the root,
Man's very voice is stilled on Troas' shore.

In Lacedæmon, loved of heroes hoar,
   No trumpet sounds, but piping shepherd's flute,
Thus have the gods ordained forevermore !

And thou, the cause, through Aphrodite's lore,
   Unblamed, art praised on poet's lyre and lute—
Man's very voice is stilled on Troas' shore.
   Thus have the gods ordained forevermore !

VILLANELLE TO THE DAFFODIL.

O DAFFODIL, flower saffron-gowned,
   Effulgent with the Sun-god's gold,
Thou bring'st the joyous season round!

While yet the earth is blanched and browned
   Thou dost thy amber leaves unfold,
O daffodil, flower saffron-gowned.

We see thee by yon mossy mound
   Wave from thy stalks each pennon bold,—
Thou bring'st the joyous season round!.

Fair child of April, promise-crowned,
   We longed for thee when winds were cold,
O daffodil, flower saffron-gowned.

Again we hear the merry sound
   Of sweet birds singing love-songs old,—
Thou bring'st the joyous season round!

Again we feel our hearts rebound
   With pleasures by thy birth foretold,—
O daffodil, flower saffron-gowned,
   Thou bring'st the joyous season round!

CUPID AND THE SHEPHERD.

(SESTINA.)

ONE merry morn when all the earth was bright,
   And flushed with dewy dawn's encrimsoning ray,
A shepherd youth, o'er whose fair face the light
   Of rosy smiles was ever wont to stray,
Roamed through a level grassy mead, bedight
   With springtime blossoms, fragrant, fresh, and gay.

But now, alas! his mood was far from gay;
   And musing how the dark world would be bright
Could he but win his maiden's love, and stray
   With her forever, basking in its light,
He saw afar, in morn's bright-beaming ray,
   A lissome boy with archers' arms bedight.

The boy shot arrows at a tree bedight
   With red-winged songsters warbling sweet and gay

CUPID AND THE SHEPHERD.

Amid the leaves and blossoms blooming bright.
    He seemed an aimless, wandering waif astray,
And so the shepherd caught him, stealing light,
    While from his eyes he flashed an angry ray.

The fair boy plead until a kindly ray
    Shone o'er the shepherd's clouded brow, bedight
With clustering locks, and he said, smiling gay,
    "I prithee promise, by thy face so bright,
To ne'er again, where'er thou mayest stray,
    Slay the sweet birds that make so glad the light."

While yet he spake, from out those eyes a light
    Divine shot forth, before whose glowing ray
The shepherd quailed, it was so wondrous bright;
    Then well he knew 'twas Cupid coy and gay,
With all his arts and subtle wiles bedight,
    And knelt in homage lest the boy should stray.

"Rise," said the God, "and ere thy footsteps stray,
    Know that within her eyes where beamed no light
Of love for thee, I will implant a ray.
    She shall be thine with all her charms bedight."

The shepherd kissed Love's hand, then bounded gay
   To gain his bliss,—and all the world was bright.

When naught is bright to those that sadly stray,
   Ofttimes a single ray of Eros' light
Will make all earth bedight with radiance gay.

ON RECEIVING A PLAQUE OF APPLE-BLOSSOMS IN WINTER.

(HUITAIN.)

For me these apple-blossoms bloom,
   Fair May flowers in this time of snow.
(How fragrant was the sweet perfume
   Of those rare buds of long ago!)
   You are the saint that made them blow,
That wrought the miracle of time,
   And, for your pinky blooms a-row,
Accept this tiny flower of rhyme.

ON A PICTURE OF ORPHEUS PLAYING BEFORE PLUTO.

(DIZAIN.)

A GLOOMY hall, dim-lit by tongues of fire,
   The stern-browed king upon his ebon throne,
And at his side, her face flushed with desire,
   Pale Proserpine, her mother long left lone ;
   Before the two, his curling locks breeze-blown,
The Jove-sent man with God-wrought lyre divine,
Nigh Tantalus, forgetful of sweet wine,
   And Sisyphus of toil severe but vain,
Too, Ixion, votive at the Orphean shrine,
   A moment eased of never-ceasing pain.

KING BOREAS.

(CHANT ROYAL.)

I SIT enthroned 'mid icy wastes afar,
   Beyond the level land of endless snow,
For months I see the brilliant polar star
   Shine on a shore, the lonelier none may know.
Supreme I rule in monarchy of might,—
My realms are boundless as the realms of Night.
   Proud court I hold, and tremblingly obey
   My many minions from the isles of Day;
And when my heralds sound aloud, behold
   My slaves appear with suppliant heads alway!
I am great Boreas, King of wind and cold.

I am the God of all the winds that are!
   I blow where'er I list,—I come, I go.
Athwart the sky upon my cloud-capped car
   I rein my steeds, swift-prancing to and fro.

The dreary woodlands shudder in affright
To hear my clarion on the mountain height.
    The sobbing sea doth moan in pain, and pray,
    "Is there no refuge from the storm-king's sway?"
I am as aged as the earth is old,
    Yet strong am I although my locks are gray;—
I am great Boreas, King of wind and cold.

I loose my chains, and then with awful jar
    And presage of disaster and dire woe,
Out rush the storms and sound the clash of war
    'Gainst all the earth, and shrill their bugles blow.
I bid them haste; they bound in eager flight
Toward far fair lands, where'er the sun's warm light
    Makes mirth and joyance; there, in rude affray,
    They trample down, despoil, and crush, and slay.
They turn green meadows to a desert wold,
    And naught for rulers of the earth care they;—
I am great Boreas, King of wind and cold.

When in the sky, a lambent scimitar,
    In early eve Endymion's bride doth glow,

KING BOREAS.

When night is perfect, and no cloud doth mar
    The peace of nature, when the river's flow
Is soft and musical, and when the sprite
Whispers to lovers on each breeze bedight
    With fragrance, then I steal forth, as I may,
    And seize upon whate'er I will for prey.
I see the billows high as hilltops rolled,
    And clutch and flaunt aloft the snowy spray!
I am great Boreas, King of wind and cold.

I am in league with Death. When I unbar
    My triple-guarded doors, and there bestow
Upon my frost-fiends freedom, bid them scar
    The brightest dales with summer blooms a-row,
They breathe on every bower a deadly blight,
And all is sere and withered in their sight.
    Unheeded now, Apollo's warming ray
    Wakes not the flower, for my chill breezes play
Where once soft zephyrs swayed the marigold,
    And where his jargon piped the noisy jay,—
I am great Boreas, King of wind and cold.

ENVOY.

O Princes, hearken what my trumpets say!—
"Man's life is naught, no mortal lives for aye;
　His might hath empire only of the mold."
Boast not yourselves, ye fragile forms of clay!
　I am great Boreas, King of wind and cold.

SONNETS.

THE LUTE PLAYER.

ONE night there came an ardent lute player,
   Who, standing by an open casement long,
   Poured forth rapt strains of such melodious song
That all the flowers with passion seemed to stir.
The birds were wakened in the somber fir,
   But no sound rose from out the gathering throng;
   And, purified from every sense of wrong,
Each man became a speechless worshipper.

Then o'er my soul a sudden thought there swept
   Of the young harper, who, without a fear,
     Played in the court to soothe the heart of Saul;
And, as the moonlight through the lattice crept,
   I seemed to see before me, ghostly clear,
     A jewelled javelin quivering in the wall!

DAWN.

The star-eyed Night along her highway dim
    Hath stolen away ; and now the dewy hush
    Is broken by the sweet, clear-noted thrush
Outpouring on the air a thankful hymn.
Above the eastern forest, tall and trim,
    The rosy goddess shows her waking blush ;
    The roguish blackbird, from a swaying rush,
Calls to his mate upon the willow slim.

And now the cattle hark to hear afar
    The shepherd dog's quick bark adown the glade.
The early riser marks the morning star
    Before the coming brightness slowly fade ;
The moon shines wan, with furrow, seam, and scar,
    Till Dawn is smitten by Apollo's blade.

TWILIGHT.

With march triumphant, Day hath speeded by;
  His banners still are floating in the west,
  Where wearied feet and tired hands may rest
When toil shall cease, and clamorous noise shall die.
E 'en now a veil is shrouding from the eye
  The towering hill tops that the woods invest,
  The sky-kissed belfry where the gray swifts nest,
And fields where waves the yet ungarnered rye.

Soft-footed Twilight, thine the subtle art
  To turn the thoughts of men to things divine,
To touch a tender chord within the heart
  That vibrates but to feelings chaste and fine;
When thou o'ershadowest earth, we stand apart
  Within a realm of peace and calm benign.

MOONRISE.

On yester night I saw Selene rise,
    What time true lovers breathe their tender vows,
    In garden-closes, 'neath the perfumed boughs,
Where low-voiced song-birds utter plaintive cries;
Her face was radiant, and, in golden wise,
    A bright crown shone upon her beaming brows.
    Athwart the purple sky, where winds carouse,
The milky-way led up to Paradise.

'Twas thus, so say the chronicles of eld,
Endymion the Goddess first beheld
    Upon a blissful eve in Arcady;
And love for her, from that enthralling hour,
Grew in his heart, as grows some crimson flower
    That tropic breezes woo eternally.

MIDNIGHT.

The world is locked in sleep with perfect night.
    Gazing from out my window I behold
    The moon, a burnished bowl of gleaming gold,
Hung in mid-sky with azure wine brimmed bright.
The sentinel church-spire lifts its stately height,
    And, where the vane upon its crest is bold,
    A single wanderer from the starry fold
Shines cold and spectral with its twinkling light.

White are the roofs, in crystal garments all;
    Unheard the murmuring streamlet's rhythmic flow—
    Weird shapes upon the spotless waste of snow,
The tree trunks stand where their gaunt shadows fall.
    Blest hour of rest—gift of a hand Divine!
    What quiet, peace, tranquillity are thine!

THE COMING OF THE GODDESS.

Coy April comes, her fair face wreathed with smiles,
    Down a long vista, budding trees between ;
    The quickening sunlight glints the grasses green
And brightens all the leafless forest aisles.
A song-thrush there her onward way beguiles
    As light she treads with airy grace of mien ;
    Upon her brow, the gracile woodland queen,
Behold a wreath—to hide her roguish wiles—
Of saintly violets plucked in bosky dell
    Where yet the drift lies white on dead leaves brown.
    About her azure eyes there flits no frown,
Yet should a lover fail 't were not so well,
    For tears can mar sweet April's brightest day,
    But if Love smiles she blushes into May.

A VISION OF PAIN.

Methought there stalked from out a cavern dim
  A shape whose cheeks were red as though with shame,
  Whose panting breath was like thin spires of flame,
Gray, gaunt, and shrunken seemed each mighty limb.
I neared this form and trembling said to him,
  "Whence comest thou? I pray thee, tell thy name!
  Rests there upon thee any blight or blame
To cause thy hollow eyes and visage grim?"

He answered me in words that made my heart
Thrill as tho' stricken with a venomed dart,—
  "I am that king most wan and dolorous
That holdeth over human ills sad reign,
  My house is one of sorrows plenteous,
Men dread my silent step,—for I am Pain!"

AT EASTER VESPERS.

As from the glow on bright Day's western walls
   The wealth of crimson glory slowly fades,
   And gray Dusk drops her mantle of soft shades,
We hear the organ's low, sweet intervals.
And, like the murmur of far waterfalls
   In summer's verdant, bough-o'erhanging glades,
   The exultant voices of the choiring maids
Float down the dim cathedral's vaulted halls.

On wings of song are borne our deathless souls
   Through boundless ether, bursting earthly bars,
We see the heavenly bands with gold citoles,
   Their brows adorned with spotless nenuphars.
The music dies,—a vesper bell out-tolls ;
   We seek the night ;—above shine clear—the stars !

DISCOVERY.

WHAT hast thou seen in Ethel's tender eyes?
   An altar sacred as Dodona's shrine?
   Or canst thou in their darkling depths divine
A host of vague and subtle mysteries,
A witching power that never latent lies,
   But warms the blood like rare Falernian wine—
   A lustrous gleam as from the stars that shine
At frosty midnight in the sapphire skies?

Ah! I have found them beaming beacon lights
   Upon the shore where grim Temptation stands,
Guiding my feet away from rocky heights,
   And warning me against engulfing sands;
Leading me onward toward the pure delights
   That wait for those who follow love's commands.

A LOCK OF HAIR.

Within my hand I hold a lock of hair,
   Dark brown, with velvet ribbon loosely tied—
   I seem to see a small, sweet face, blue-eyed,
A fair young form to me far more than fair;
The rosy lips—a merry, pouting pair—
   In roguish smile forever seem to bide,
   Half-veiling pearls more white than those that hide
In many-caverned ocean's darkest lair.

This, of all pictures that the bastioned keep
   Of memory holds, the dearest do I prize;
The vision fair, engraven clear and deep
   Upon my heart of hearts, Madonna-wise,
Unfolds to me, as doth Lethean sleep,
   A glimpse, a gleam of some bright paradise!

LE ROI EST MORT, VIVE LE ROI.

He who hath known the dreary courts of pain
   Grows glad at heart to feel the refluent breath
   Of airs unburdened by the germs of death,
From spicy isles beyond the moaning main ;
So we who know the pallid Winter's reign
   Rejoice to hearken what the March wind saith
   As down the dales it wildly wantoneth,
And sweeps across the ice-encumbered plain.

Whene'er a monarch lieth calm and cold
   Beneath all-conquering Death's remorseless sting,
   The brazen bells, in consonant peal, outring
Unto the heir their greetings manifold ;
   Thus let us welcome our new sovereign, Spring,
   And cry, "The king is dead, long live the king!"

PRISCILLA.

As trippingly as any bird in spring
   She speeds across the newly fallen snow ;
   I see the wanton wintry breezes blow
Her fair brown locks that round her forehead cling,
And kiss her dewy lips, sweet murmuring,
   And touch each cheek, a budding Jacqueminot.
   The dreary earth takes on a brighter glow,
Her presence is a joy to every thing.

Yet seems she meek and shy and so demure,
   With air of noble breeding, chaste and fine,
   That they who chance her peaceful face to scan,
Declare her one whose every thought is pure,
   Not stern like those of her unbending line,
   But a time-tempered, lovely Puritan.

AGANIPPE.

She heard the fluting wind amid the trees
    Whene'er she stood, at morn or moonlit night,
    Beside her fountain sparkling silvery bright,
And saw approach, across the flowery leas,
The pilgrim bards who came from over seas
    To taste her cup of infinite delight ;
    For whoso drank, his songs, in loftier flight,
Soared to the skies like choral symphonies.

But now no nymph stands warder o'er the fount
That bubbles 'neath the Heliconian mount ;
    The lyre is voiceless by the Grecian main.
And since I may not drain the inspiring draught
That the divine Hellenian lyrists quaffed,
    I strive to scale the heights of song in vain !

www.ingramcontent.com/pod-product-compliance
Lightning Source LLC
Chambersburg PA
CBHW030355170426
43202CB00010B/1377